FE 19

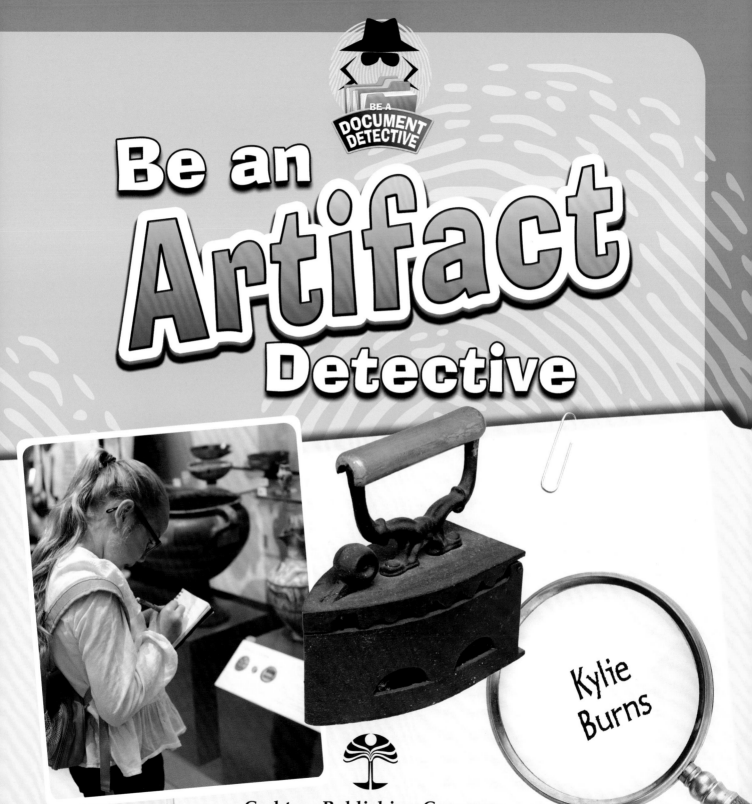

BE A
DOCUMENT
DETECTIVE

Be an Artifact Detective

Kylie Burns

Crabtree Publishing Company

www.crabtreebooks.com

BE A
DOCUMENT DETECTIVE

Author: Kylie Burns

Series research and development: Reagan Miller

Editorial director: Kathy Middleton

Editors: Janine Deschenes, Reagan Miller

Proofreader: Petrice Custance

Design: Margaret Amy Salter

Photo research: Abigail Smith

Production coordinator and prepress technician:
  Abigail Smith

Print coordinator: Margaret Amy Salter

Photographs:

iStock: PeopleImages, p 8; scorpion56, p 10; chrisbrignell, p 14 (bottom left); ideabug, p 14 (middle right)

Shutterstock: © Pen_85, p 15; © Denys Prykhodov, p 19 (right)

Wikimedia Commons: Creative Commons, p 22

All other images from Shutterstock

Library and Archives Canada Cataloguing in Publication

Burns, Kylie, author
      Be an artifact detective / Kylie Burns.

(Be a document detective)
Includes index.
Issued in print and electronic formats.
ISBN 978-0-7787-3039-2 (hardcover).--
ISBN 978-0-7787-3080-4 (softcover).--ISBN 978-1-4271-1870-7 (HTML)

      1. History--Research--Juvenile literature. 2. History--Sources--Juvenile literature. 3. History--Methodology--Juvenile literature. 4. Antiquities--Juvenile literature. 5. Material culture--Juvenile literature. I. Title.

D16.B9655 2017   j907.2   C2016-907105-7
                                           C2016-907106-5

Library of Congress Cataloging-in-Publication Data

Names: Burns, Kylie, author.
Title: Be an artifact detective / Kylie Burns.
Description: New York, New York : Crabtree Publishing Company, 2017. |
Series: Be a document detective | Includes index.
Identifiers: LCCN 2017007119 (print) | LCCN 2017021546 (ebook) |
    ISBN 9781427118707 (Electronic HTML) |
    ISBN 9780778730392 (reinforced library binding : alkaline paper) |
    ISBN 9780778730804 (paperback : alkaline paper)
Subjects: LCSH: Archaeology--Methodology--Juvenile literature. |
    Antiquities--Collection and preservation--Juvenile literature. |
    Historiography--Methodology--Juvenile literature. | History--Sources--
    Juvenile literature.
Classification: LCC CC75 (ebook) | LCC CC75 .B87 2017 (print) |
    DDC 930.1--dc23
LC record available at https://lccn.loc.gov/2017007119

Crabtree Publishing Company

www.crabtreebooks.com   1-800-387-7650

Printed in Canada/062017/MA20170420

Published in Canada
Crabtree Publishing
616 Welland Ave.
St. Catharines, Ontario
L2M 5V6

Published in the United States
Crabtree Publishing
PMB 59051
350 Fifth Avenue, 59th Floor
New York, New York 10118

Published in the United Kingdom
Crabtree Publishing
Maritime House
Basin Road North, Hove
BN41 1WR

Published in Australia
Crabtree Publishing
3 Charles Street
Coburg North
VIC 3058

Contents

The Mystery of History

Do you wonder what life was like hundreds of years ago? In this book, you will learn to ask and answer questions about the past. History is the study of things that happened in the past. It tells about people and places, and how they have changed over time.

History Detectives

Historians are people who study history. They learn about people, places, and events from the past. Just like a detective searches for clues to solve a mystery, a historian looks for clues to answer questions about the past. Historians look for answers to questions such as:

- **How did people in the past live their daily lives?**
- **How do things that happened in the past affect us today?**
- **What has changed or stayed the same over time?**

What are Primary Sources?

What do an old tool, a map, and a diary have in common? They are all **primary sources**. Primary sources are records created by people during a certain time in history. They give **eyewitness** information about people, places, and events.

Maps are a type of primary source. They can teach us about how different places looked long ago.

A letter is a primary source that gives a record of a person's daily life.

Clues to the Past

Historians study letters, maps, and other primary sources to look for clues about the past. They use what they learn as **evidence** to support their answers to questions about the people, places, and events from long ago.

This funny-looking object is called a **gramophone**. It was used to play music more than 100 years ago.

How are Artifacts Helpful?

Primary sources include **artifacts** which are objects that people made, used, and left behind. Artifacts help us make connections to people and events of the past because they show us things that were important to people long ago. Clothing, tools, and coins are all examples of artifacts.

Some families pass down artifacts, such as jewelry, from **generation** to generation. Studying family artifacts helps us learn about the members of a family and the things that were important to them.

Many Kinds of Primary Sources

Historians ask questions about many different kinds of primary sources, including artifacts. Studying only one primary source does not give historians enough evidence to find answers. They use what they already know about a time period and a place to help them understand how an artifact was made and used by people long ago.

This airplane is a toy children played with many years ago. It is different from toys today because it is made of wood.

Detective Duty!

How is the spinning top shown above different from the toys you play with today?

Toys are artifacts that give us clues about how children in different times played, what they enjoyed, and how toys are different or the same today.

Where in the World are Artifacts?

Artifacts are everywhere! They come from different times in history and are found in different places. Some of the oldest artifacts come from the ground! These artifacts are dug up by scientists called **archaeologists**. Archaeologists dig for artifacts in places where people lived long ago.

Archaeologists use tools such as shovels and hammers to dig up artifacts from the ground. Archaeologists have found many tools, cooking pots, and even toys that are thousands of years old.

Looking Closer

Archaeologists share the artifacts they have found with the world. They show them through photos, posting information online, and by giving them to museums. This gives everyone a chance to learn about artifacts. Museums display artifacts carefully to keep them from being damaged. At some museums, you can see, feel, smell, and hear artifacts yourself!

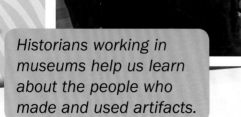

Historians working in museums help us learn about the people who made and used artifacts.

Questions and Answers

Historians ask questions to find out how an artifact was made, and what it was used for. Answering these questions can help them find out about the way people lived or worked during a certain time period. Some questions may not be answered at all. But, every piece of information helps. These are often the first questions historians ask:

- What is it? What do you notice about how it looks, such as its color or size?

- What materials is it made from? How do you think it was made?

- Who used it, and how was it used?

- What other questions do I have?

Does this artifact look like something you have seen or used? What do you think it was used for?

Yesterday and Today

Artifacts in museums, in books, and on the Internet often have labels. Labels include details about an artifact that people may not know just by looking at it. They often give details such as the name of the artifact, where it was found, and when it was made. This information may come from the people who discovered the artifact, or historians working at a museum.

This girl is learning more about an artifact from its label.

Some artifacts have the date printed on them, such as this coin from the year 1907.

Looking Closer

Artifact detectives learn by asking questions about an artifact and studying it closely. They notice things such as the size and shape of the artifact. It may look like something we use today. They search for clues to make connections to a time and place in history. Look closely at the artifacts below. What do they tell you about what schools were like many years ago?

- This is a small bench with a desk attached.

- This artifact is made of wood. It looks hard to sit on.

- It has a place to sit, and a place to write, just like my desk at school. I think this was a student's desk a long time ago.

- I wonder if every desk looked like this at schools long ago.

- This is a small chalkboard with chalk. It has wood on the outside.

- It looks much smaller than the chalkboards in classrooms today.

- I wonder if students each had one to write on.

- Is this small chalkboard the only thing students had to write on? What was it called? Did they only write with chalk?

Learning More

It's normal to have unanswered questions when studying artifacts. What questions about the artifacts were you not able to answer? To answer these questions, you can find more information at the library, on the Internet, or by talking to a historian at a museum.

Back to Basics

When we study artifacts, we learn more about how people long ago met their **basic needs**. Basic needs are the things people need to survive, or stay alive. Basic needs include shelter, food, water, and clothing.

This house was built more than 130 years ago. It shows how some people living during that time met their basic need for shelter.

Research this!

We can learn how cooking tools helped people prepare food, how building tools helped create shelter, and how clothing was made to protect people from heat or cold. Look closely at the artifact below and think about the questions on page 12. How many can you answer? Do we use anything that looks similar today?

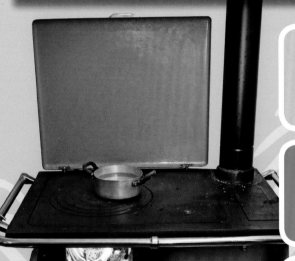

This artifact is shaped like a large box. It has four doors with handles and fire inside. It looks like there is an open lid on top.

The artifact looks like it is made from strong metal. It looks like it was made with machines, not by hand.

There are handles for people to open and close the doors. A pot sits on top of the artifact. Maybe the fire inside heats up food.

I wonder how the fire is lit. Does food cook on top only, or can you put it inside one of the doors?

Detective Duty!

What basic need do you think this artifact met for people in the past?

Changing Times

Studying artifacts can help us learn how things change over time. Change happens when people develop new ways of doing things and new tools to use. These tools are known as **technology.** Technology changes over time to create better, faster ways of doing work. Artifacts can show changes in technology over time. They show how the tools people used to do a task have changed.

Computer Technology

A computer is a type of technology that helps people do work. Today's computers are more powerful than ever. But they did not start out that way!

Seeing Big Changes

Sometimes technology changes a little over time. Often, it changes a lot. Look at each artifact below and answer the questions. To start, notice the size and number of parts you see in these artifacts. Notice how they are different or the same from the computer technology you use today. How has computer technology changed over time?

- What do you notice about each artifact?

- Which computer do you think was made first?

- What clues tell you the period of time in which each artifact was created?

- Who do you think used each of these technologies? How was each used?

- What do you still want to know?

Detective Duty!

Name one way each artifact shows a change in computer technology.

19

Tomorrow's Artifacts

Everything made and used by people today can one day become an artifact. Think about things you and your family use at school, at home, and at work. How would the objects you and your family use give information about how you live today?

Challenge!

Choose three objects that you use every day. Choose one from school, one from home, and one type of technology that you use every day. These objects are artifacts that teach others about your life today. Explain why you chose those artifacts. How do they give clues about your daily life? What do you think future artifact detectives might learn about you by studying them?

Your favorite chair at home is an artifact. It gives clues about the materials you find comfortable, the activities you like to do in it, such as reading books or playing video games, and what furniture looks like today.

That's a Wrap

What were the objects you chose as artifacts? Share your choices and reasons with a classmate. How were your artifacts the same or different? Do you think historians of the future will understand the objects we use today?

Time Capsule

Have you ever heard of a **time capsule**? A time capsule contains artifacts and information from an earlier time and is saved or hidden for people in the future to find. Some time capsules include letters and photographs along with artifacts. When someone finds a time capsule, they get to see, feel, smell, and hear artifacts from the past.

This is an example of a time capsule. This time capsule is being put inside a bridge!

Learning More

There are many places you can visit to find out more about primary sources. Start with your local museum and library. Churches, community groups, and schools are also good places to find information.

These books and websites will help you learn more:

Books

Duke, Kate. *Archaeologists Dig for Clues.* HarperCollins Children's Books, 1996.

Panchyk, Richard. *Archaeology for Kids: Uncovering the Mysteries of our Past.* Chicago Review Press, 2001.

Stewart, Melissa. *Titanic.* National Geographic Society, 2012.

Websites

www.dkfindout.com/us/history/
This site contains exciting facts, photos of ancient artifacts, and fun interactive games.

www.history.org/kids/
Check out this site from the Colonial Williamsburg Foundation. It contains cool facts and interactive activities about daily life in the past. It even has an online tour of the historic town of Colonial Williamsburg.

http://kids.canadashistory.ca/Kids/Home.aspx
Visit this site for facts about Canadian history and artifacts, as well as puzzles, quizzes, and contests.

Words to Know

archaeologist | A scientist who searches and digs for artifacts from the past
artifact | An object that people created or used
basic needs | The things people need to survive, such as food, shelter, water, and clothing
evidence | Information, items, and facts that help answer questions
eyewitness | A person who sees something happen and can tell us about it
generation | People living at the same time, of the same age. In a family, three generations would describe a grandmother, a mother, and a daughter.
gramophone | A device that plays music on records
historian | A person who studies the past
primary source | Objects, letters, maps, and photographs that were created by people in the past
technology | The tools people use to do work, which change and improve over time
time capsule | A container that holds artifacts from the past for people in the future to learn from

Index

About the Author:

Kylie Burns is a writer and teacher. She has written several children's books on a wide range of interesting topics. She loves researching primary sources. Once, she even discovered some of her ancestors' personal artifacts, letters, and photos on display in a museum!